SPLIT INFINI

THREE WAY

By Alexander Millington

[signature]   *[signature]*

Naomi

Published by Playdead Press 2021

© Alexander Millington 2021

Alexander Millington has asserted his rights under the Copyright, Design and Patents Act, 1988, to be identified as the author of this work.

A CIP catalogue record for this book is available from the British Library.

ISBN 978-1-910067-93-2

Playdead Press
www.playdeadpress.com

THREE WAY was first performed at the Lion & Unicorn Theatre, London, on 24 August 2021, as part of the Camden Fringe Festival. The cast was as follows:

ONE   Alexander Millington

TWO   Jamie Dunn

THREE   Naomi Phillips

Director   Helen Millington
Additional Direction   Alexander Millington
Technical Design   Pete Clarke

Cast and Creatives

Alexander Millington | Writer/Performer

Alexander is Co-Creative Director of Split Infinitive. He has previously produced work through his previous company, Conceptual Arts Theatre Company Ltd, which has been performed at the Stockwell Playhouse, Guildhall Arts Centre, New Theatre Royal Lincoln and Lincoln Performing Arts Centre. He was commissioned by New Project Theatre for a new writing festival in Coventry. Alexander is a Licentiate of Trinity College London and holds an MA in Playwriting from the University of Lincoln. Alexander is acknowledged in the True Acting Institutes Best Ten Minute Plays of 2019 for his play, *Window Shopping*. His other credits include *A Real Christmas* (2020) and *Over Time* (2020) broadcast on BBC Radio. Alexander has also collaborated on works with the American Dramatist Guild and New Works Playhouse.

Jamie Dunn | Performer

Jamie's previous credits include working with Conceptual Arts Theatre Company's production of *The Concept of Love* (2016), *The Understudies*

(2017) and *The Impossible Dream* (2017). He has previously played Henry in *Henry V* (2014), Robbie Hart in *The Wedding Singer* (2014) and Luke in *Christmas is Miles Away* (2015). In addition to his theatre work, Jamie has also appeared in the short films *Botch Up* (2018), *The Bright Side* (2017), *The Chest* (2017) and *Static Rainbow* (2015) with production company, Plastic Grenade.

Naomi Phillips | Performer

Naomi has received numerous awards from various drama festivals. At the 2019 Lincoln Music and Drama Festival, she received first place in the sonnet selection and Tennyson selection, second place in the dramatic selection and third in lyric and verse. At the 2018 Lincoln Festival she received first place in the Shakespearean selection and sonnet selection, and also achieved second place for her individual dramatic selection. At the 2019 Wolfit Festival of Drama, Music and Verse Speaking in Newark she received first place for her Shakespeare solo performance and first place for her dramatic solo performance. Following completion of her A Levels, Naomi has been working towards achieving a place at drama school. Performing in Three Way is Naomi's first professional production outside of festivals.

Helen Millington | Director

Helen is Co-Artistic Director of Split Infinitive, directing their previous performances. Helen has previously performed with Lincoln Shakespeare Company, Indulgence Theatre, The Lincoln Mystery Plays and has directed various productions including devised performances and children's theatre. Alongside Split Infinitive, Helen runs Lincoln School of Speech and Drama, is Secretary of The Lincoln Music & Drama Festival, was Head of Speech & Drama at Stamford Endowed Schools, and has adjudicated many poetry competitions. She is a member of the Society of Teachers of Speech and Drama and holds an MA in Contemporary British Theatre from the University of Lincoln. Through Split Infinitive, Helen has also previously worked on R&D sessions for projects including *I am an actor…* (2020), *Over Time* (2020), *Jump, Jump, Push* (2019), *New Year, Same Me* (2019), and *Child's Play* (2018).

Pete Clarke | Technical Designer

Pete has previously worked as a lighting designer and technician on *Dance For China* (2015), *Once Upon A Time* (2014) and *Canterbury Tales* (2014). He has additionally worked as a lighting and sound technician for *Someone Else's Daughter* (2013). He has also acted as a lighting technician on *The Boom Room* (2007-2008) and on *The Pirates of Penzance* (2006).

Split Infinitive

Split Infinitive is a Lincolnshire based theatre company dedicated to creating original theatre, which explores the dynamics between spectator and performer and examines the relationships created throughout our lives. Established is 2019, Split Infinitive has worked with local and emerging artists whilst developing new work. Since 2019, they have collaborated with other theatre companies to create engaging online performances including two performances broadcast on BBC Radio (*A Real Christmas* and *Over Time*). Three Way is Split Infinitive's first professional live production since establishing themselves.

Twitter	@SplitTheatre
Facebook	@SplitInfinitiveTheatre
Instagram	@SplitInfinitiveTheatre
Online	www.splitinfinitivetheatre.co.uk

SPLIT INFINITIVE

Acknowledgements

Special thanks go to;

Lonely Penguin, who provided us with a platform during the early stages of script development.

Joe Staton and his group WReAct: Write, Read and Act who brought together an audience of knowledgeable theatre goers to provide feedback.

Ecce Homo for kindly providing us with costume items for the production.

Lewis Ranshaw for generously offering his time and assistance with our marketing material.

And a final thank you to everyone who attended our scripted reading and offered such kind words of encouragement and support: Mary-Jane Ives, Cathy Ashwin, Lewis Ranshaw, Frankie Buttery, Gray Lowes, Angela Wood, Sarah Baish, Mike 'The Fox' Belcher and Ange Edwards.

Extra thanks go to Cassius Carbonara.

THREE WAY

Alexander Millington

CHARACTERS

One, *male*
Two, *male*
Three, *female*

As the audience enter, they will be greeted by the cast, who will make conversation. Throughout each monologue there are a series of questions. These questions can be delivered either rhetorically or directly to the audience. If directed at the audience, then the questions should become increasingly intimate as the monologues progress. Where [NAME] is stated in the text, this should be the real name of an audience member, elicited from them by the character.

This text went to press before the end of rehearsals and may differ from the play as performed.

One enters. He appears a little exhausted and dishevelled. The sound of a TV is heard before he turns it off.

One   "Did you do it? How was it? Did she make you cum?" Nothing like a Nazi style interrogation as soon as you walk through the door. No kiss hello as I walk in, no, "Hey hun, how's it going? What do you fancy for tea?" Just straight out with it. But that's Chris for you, I knew he wouldn't be cool about it.

It had been a while since I'd slept with someone new. So, when... (*To female audience member*) I'm sorry, what's your name? (*Waits for audience members name*) Thank you. (*As before*) So, when [NAME] took me up to her bedroom, as excited as I was, I was more nervous than anything. I don't think I'd even seen a naked woman since I was about 18 or something. In the flesh anyway.

13

Obviously, I'd seen them in films and things, but...
well, it's a bit different close up isn't it? It's like that
naked dating show on TV. You've seen a naked
body before, you know what to expect, you know
how it all works and then suddenly... the clothes are
off. Wow! I think the fact that [NAME] and I had
known each other for years is actually what made it
worse. Not the sex. Just that initial... "So, that's
your vagina." You know. I mean, how do you
respond to seeing someone's vagina? Or penis for
that matter? In either case, they're not exactly the
most attractive part of a person's body. Not unless
you're really lucky... or unlucky I suppose.
Anyway, the actual sex part was fine. More than
fine. I guess that was the problem really.

I told him it was fine. "Fine!" he snaps at me.
"Fine's no good. The doctor said that if you both

enjoy it and both climax together it improves her chances of fertility. Fine is not good!" He said, "Well, if it hasn't worked this time, you'll just have to go and do it again, won't you!" Is it just me, or is there something about pre-prescribed sex that's just so... unsexy? It's like enforced fun. I mean, what if it hasn't worked? Then when I try again... if I try again, then that's all I'm going to be thinking about now. Then I definitely won't be able to enjoy it. Not that I don't like thinking about Chris when I'm... but... well, you know.

You know when you're asleep, and you have a sex dream? Are you having sex with the person you're with? Your husband, your wife, boyfriend, girlfriend, whatever? I'm not. I never have. Dreams are a bit like porn really, aren't they? They're fantasies. Make believe. No matter how much you want to believe that the 'amateur' couple in the video are actually a couple in real life, and that this is their actual sex, doesn't make it true. And it's the same for dreams I think, sex dreams anyway, at least it is for me. I mean, so what if your subconscious wants to see the trolley pusher from M&S fuck you in the middle of your local gym. Or if it wants you to cum over the chest of a young Richard Gere as he turns into your old geography teacher. Or if it wants you to make your husband's best friend cum until she can't bear it anymore, whilst he sits in the corner, cheering you on, with tears running down his face. It's just a dream, isn't it? It doesn't mean anything.

Pause.

Chris and I first met when we were at Uni. I was studying journalism, he was doing a performing arts degree. We met at one of the freshers' events in the first week. Apparently, he clocked me straight away, but was too shy to come over and say anything. He likes to tell it that way because it makes it sound like it was love at first sight. However, the only reason we even spoke that night was because he was wearing the tightest jeans and his arse looked fucking phenomenal. I wasn't letting that get away from me. And I didn't. I wasn't looking for a relationship. I'd just moved away from home. The first week of the start of my new life. To finally be who I wanted to be. I just wanted to fuck and have fun. He just happened to be one of the people I fucked and had fun with. You can sort of see why he likes to tell it his way. It is a touch more romantic, I guess.

By the time the Christmas holidays had arrived, we'd already decided to be 'exclusive', whatever that means. His suggestion. He says that during those first couple of months, when we were just having fun, that he hadn't slept with anyone else, which I know is a lie because David, one of the guys on my course, said that Chris gave him head in the library toilet. I don't mind that he did. I fooled around loads during those first few months. Guys, girls, sometimes both. It's what Uni's for, isn't it? But again, it ruins the romance of the story for Chris. I was always getting more action than him, which I think was making him a little jealous. My experimental phase, he calls it.

He proposed to me in our final year. Caught me a little off guard if I'm honest. Halfway through a dissertation, desperately trying to concentrate and suddenly someone asks you to dedicate the rest of your life to them. Now, I love Chris, loved, love, but I wasn't quite ready to settle down. But then, what would happen if I said "no"? Why is it, that when someone asks you to marry them, if you say "no", then straight away it's seen as a breakup? I didn't want to break up. If I had wanted a breakup, I'd have asked for a breakup. I just wasn't ready yet. I sometimes wonder, what if I hadn't said yes?

Two enters. He is wearing a towel as if he has just got out of the shower. Throughout the monologue he is getting dressed as if going on a date.

Two   (*To male audience member.*) I'm sorry, what's your name? (*Waits for audience members name*) Thank you. (*As before*) I first met [NAME] online. I'm, well I was, fairly new to the whole... you know... online dating thing before I met him. I mean I had a

Tinder and Grindr account and everything, but I'd never met up with anyone. But I just saw his picture and thought he was kind of cute, so I sent him a message and that was it really.

Ok, I know it wasn't exactly like other online dating sites, but hey, who cares.

He adjusts his towel.

I don't feel ashamed about anything. Why should I? If I'm sat at home, and I know I'm not the only one, if you're at home right, and you fancy something to eat, but you haven't got anything in or you can't be bothered to cook, you go online don't you? We've all done it. Cheeky Nando's mid-week, courtesy of Deliveroo, I thank you. Naughty Chinese on a Saturday night thanks to the easy-to-use Just Eat – Hungry House for you city folk.

We've all done it. It's the way we live now. If you want something that you can't be arsed to sort yourself, you pay someone to sort it for you.

I've never been good at dating. There's always so much pressure, right? Particularly when you don't know them. Do I look alright? Do I smell alright? Do they fancy me? Do I have something stuck in my teeth? Do they want to sleep with me? Are they into anything weird? Are they gonna be any good? If I go to theirs do I stay the night, or will they kick me out? If they come back to mine will they just fuck me and run?

In an age where everyone is suffering with anxiety and stress and depression, why the fuck should I have to worry about all that shit?

He drops his towel to the floor and walks away to the back of the stage.

I hadn't actually been with many guys before [NAME]. Only a few. Well, one.

He begins to pull on a pair of underwear.

He was a friend of a friend. My mate didn't know I was into guys, but his friend said he could tell a mile off. Thanks! Anyway, I took his addy for MSN, as you did in the old days, and added him when I got home. I dunno how we got onto it, but he was talking about this guy he'd been with. Still pretending I wasn't interested, I asked him what it was like. Next thing I know I've invited him round, with some line like "I never wanted to do stuff with a guy, but if you tried anything I probably wouldn't stop you", you know, just acting as if I'm only gonna do it to be polite to him. We've all done stuff just to be polite right? It's not just me.

Anyway, he came round and we're in my bedroom. I don't know who made the first move or how it happened, all I can remember is we were kissing. Then his shirt was off. Then my shirt was off. Things seemed to move really quickly from jeans being on, to jeans being off. He was laid on top of me and I could feel him… inside his boxers, pressing against me.

Two things: number one, his boxers were hideous, I mean seriously! Light blue, baggy, old and worn out, George at Asda kind of boxers. If someone invites you round basically guaranteeing you that something is going to happen, you'd wear nice underwear, right? Not that I'm saying I had guaranteed him or anything, I just meant that…

well, I'd put on nicer boxers. Number two, and I'm sure all guys feels like this when presented in any way, shape or form with another guy's cock, the only thing running through your head is... fuck!

I'd never felt so small in my life. You suddenly begin to appreciate the naivety you feel as a guy before your first time. Your cock is the only cock in the world. There is nothing wrong with it. It is perfect! That is until you see one in the flesh that's bigger. Sure, you see them in porn, but they're professionals, they're paid to have huge dicks. He'd got me so turned on with all the kissing and touching and stuff, I was like a rock. As soon as I felt it, pressing against me through his cheap nasty Asda boxers, I was so conflicted. On one hand "Fuck me this is actually happening. This is so fucking hot!" and on the other "Fuck me, I'm so fucking small!" I'd never been so flaccid and so hard at the same time in my life. My body soon made up its mind though.

Three enters. She wears a dress that is both summery and formal. She is holding a bunch of flowers, still wrapped in their cellophane from the supermarket. Throughout the monologue, she is preparing the flowers. The bunch is made up of various different flowers, including roses.

Three   It's funny the things you remember from your childhood. Do you have things that stand out to you for no real reason? An old t-shirt, the colour of the walls in your old bedroom, the sound of the tumble dryer? We used to have this grey sofa. Grey, leather sofa. Like elephant's skin. With green felt cushions. The sofa was covered in grubby marks from sticky fingers, spilt drinks, bits of food, and it's not like my parents didn't clean it. It was just so old and warn that any dirt just seeped into the flesh of this thick skinned beast. It had that sort of ruckled up thing going on over its arms too so you could see the dust, bits of crisps, bits of dead skin trapped within the creases. It had buttons on the back of it, like it was trying to be one of those Chesterfield sofas but was failing miserably. The buttons just created more pockets for bugs to crawl into and die, like a fly elephant graveyard. It wasn't even comfortable.

Apparently I cried when they told me. I cried a lot, at least that's what they said I did. I don't remember. I do remember it was dark. Night-time. I remember that Dad was sat down, and Mum was stood up. And I'm pretty sure I was sat on that grey leather sofa with its green cushions. But I don't remember crying.

A few months after this announcement where I cried a lot but didn't, Dad moved out. I knew it was coming. As in I knew it was happening on this particular day, but it was still weird. I went to school as normal, and when I came home everything had gone, everything of his. Even the grey sofa.

Pause.

When you're a kid, your parents never really tell you anything. Nothing important or truthful anyway. They tell you lies, white lies, but still lies. They try and teach you that the world's a good place. That if you try your best you can achieve anything, and that everyone is nice. But sometimes they decide they can be happier if they're not around each other anymore. That's what Mum and Dad told me at the time anyway, as far as I remember. But that's not always true. Dad wasn't happier afterwards.

Not many parents seem to stay together these days. How many people here have parents that are still together? Hmm. Seems to be the norm now really. It's more surprising to hear if people are still together.

Mum was happier. We actually started doing things together. Not just trips to Tesco or something like that but actually doing things. We'd talk. She'd ask about school and about my friends, it was nice. When I stayed with Dad though, he always just seemed so exhausted. I'd try and suggest something like going for a walk across the fields, or through the woods, but he never wanted to. Dad always used to be wandering around out there. He was big on wildflowers. Bit of an amateur botanist. He knew all the names, even the Latin ones. Myosotis. Always a popular one. Any ideas? Myosotis. Forget-me-nots to you and me.

Mum said she'd been seeing someone new. Carl. I remember hearing Mum laugh, a lot. The house was always filled with her laughter. Suddenly Mum had become a proper little hostess, always having her girlfriends round or Carl lighting up a barbeque. When I went round to Dad's though it was always so quiet.

I can't really remember much from school, but I do remember one geography class when we were looking at Africa and its native animals, and that although elephants don't necessarily mate for life, they are really loyal animals when it comes to their families. The male elephant tends to live alone, while the female elephants stay sociable with other females and their offspring. I guess this was our family now.

One   [NAME] was a member of Chris's Drama Society. It was fucking awful going to their society parties. All screaming and singing Disney shit. Apparently [NAME] and Chris got talking because she thought he was fit and tried it on with him. I guess that's why it seems quite funny the way things turned out.

It had only been a week since that night at [NAME]'s when we decided to try again. We didn't see the point in waiting a whole month to find out if it had worked or not, so... I booked a hotel room. I thought a neutral playing field might be a bit more conducive this time, rather than one of us having the home advantage, as it were. When [NAME] arrived, she was wearing this real body hugging, green dress. She looked amazing. When we got up to the room, she took it off and had on this lingerie that just fitted and held her body perfectly. I was like a fucking rock from the moment that dress came off. I think that's when I really knew.

He takes a drink from the mini bar fridge.

[NAME] had always wanted to have kids, but no one was ever as perfect, in her eyes, as her Dad so she always ended things before it got too serious. She actually came to Chris first, asked if he would be interested in being her baby Daddy. I've never seen him go so red so quickly, his face was like a baboon's arsehole.

This prompted a whole new set of conversations for Chris and me. We'd never really spoken about kids ourselves, we were more dog people, so I was surprised when Chris started researching it. We chatted with [NAME] about adopting, but she was afraid she wouldn't feel a connection with it if it wasn't biologically hers. She thought about IVF, until we showed her the price. I said to Chris, "You'll just have to get your tip wet and get the job done yourself!", knowing full well he wouldn't be able to get it up for her, even if they did it in the dark with Hugh Jackman singing *The Greatest Showman* at him.

One morning, after a long night of Chris Googling, he asked me if I ever watched straight porn. Now, when your partner asks you something like this, is it, or is it not, nine times out of ten, a complete and utter fucking trap? I mean, so what if I did? He was never gonna watch it with me. And he knew I watched porn without him sometimes.

"Why?" I asked. "Can you still get turned on looking at women?" he replied. Apparently, the internet told him, sex between a man and woman is generally considered to be the easiest and most reliable way to make a baby. Who'd have thought. He'd spent all night online trying to find a way to help [NAME], but it basically came down to artificial insemination or actual insemination. And so essentially, he was asking why couldn't I do it instead of him?

Pause.

They say certain positions can help when conceiving. Missionary is meant to be good. Very traditional. Doggie-style too. Apparently, it allows for a deeper penetration, so the sperm has less distance to travel. I mean, we'd booked the hotel for the whole night, might as well try it as many ways as we can and improve our chances. Right?

The next morning, before we'd even left the hotel, Chris had left three messages on my phone. All asking how it went. What do you say? What are you *meant* to say when the person you love asks you how sex was with their best friend? You know when you're a little way into a relationship and you get to that point where you are discussing your previous partners, do you ever truthfully tell them about the good ones? You tell them about the bad ones, obviously. That's safe. That makes them feel good about themselves. But you don't tell the truth about the good ones. The best fucks of your life. The times when you are so turned on that you could barely keep your hands off each other. The nights when you did it three, four, five times. Of course you don't. It just creates tension. So, when he asked how it went at the hotel, I just said: "It was fine. We both came. Fingers crossed".

There wasn't anything emotional in it. I wasn't falling in love with [NAME]. I wasn't falling out of love with Chris, I don't think. The sex was just so… I missed it. Being with a woman. Ever since we got married, Chris wouldn't even talk about the fact I had been with women before him. The unspoken 'experimental phase' – the before time. If he was gay and I was married to him, then I must be gay. That's what he always said. So that's what I came to believe. But being with [NAME]… I don't find Chris any less attractive, I really don't but… I needed more.

Whatever it was we did that night, it worked. [NAME] phoned me and told me she'd taken a test and it was positive. I asked if she had told Chris yet. She said she hadn't.

Pause. He gets a drink from the mini bar.

I asked if we had to tell Chris straight away. I messaged Chris that afternoon, and said she'd taken a test... (*Pause*) and that I was going to book another night at the hotel to try again. He replied saying: "Think of me!"

Two   Now, just to clarify, I am not a confident person, I'm a bit awkward in social situations, I don't like to make a fuss and I do not invite strange guys I've only just met round to my house, get them naked and take their whole penis in my mouth in one go without even checking whether I could. But fuck me.

This is the time when I've got to say hats off to all the men and women out there in the adult film industry who have perfected the deep throat, and also the time when I warn any young guy or girl thinking about doing it for the first time, for god sake ease into it. Luckily, I don't have a gag reflex but the first time you have a nine-and-a-half-inch schlong down your throat is not the time that you want to find out you do.

Pause.

Where was I? Oh yes. Long story short, I made him cum. I was so nervous in the end that I couldn't. Then he left. And outed me to all our mutual friends by telling them about me taking his balls in my mouth while I jerked him off to climax. That was the only guy I'd been with before [NAME], not exactly the most positive of experiences.

I was almost exclusively with girls after that encounter. Usually long term relationships. A few months or a year here and there. They never really worked out though. I always feel too self-conscious. Even when I've been with someone for ages. I just feel like they're judging me. But recently, after my last break up, I just fancied something easy. No commitment, no getting self-conscious. And when you can find a way of having a date with someone you find attractive, who you know will say they find you attractive, who you know will definitely come back to the hotel room with you if you want them to, make you cum and then stay only as long as you want them to, why wouldn't you do it?

Seriously, if I gave you the option of a casual date with a stranger, where anything could go wrong, or a perfect date where you have set out the expectations beforehand, but you have to pay a little for the assurance that everything will go to plan, wouldn't you take the easy option? Don't get me wrong, I love spontaneity as much as the next guy - that's a lie, I fucking hate spontaneity, but that's not the point, sometimes you just want a sure thing. There's enough pressure in life without having to worry about whether your date's a one-nighter or a third dater, a joker or just a dick, a top or a bottom.

Pause.

He suggested the bar where we met and the restaurant where we ate. Everything else I set out. I told him I just needed to feel wanted. That I thought I might want to have sex but wasn't certain. That I hadn't had much experience, but that I did know I liked giving head. He said we could do anything. As much or as little as I wanted.

Beat. He sits down and pulls on a pair of socks.

The first night we met, after the meal... (*pause*) we went back to the hotel room and... he kissed me. He kissed me hard on the lips, his hands round the back of my neck and running through my hair. As we kissed I felt his hands on my back, running all over me. Then he stopped. He looked at me, and he asked if I was certain I wanted to do this, and I just nodded.

Three After a while, Dad seemed a little better, didn't seem as down as he had at the start of everything. He seemed to be going out more, exercising again. Sometimes the house would even smell like flowers if he'd found any interesting ones on his walk.

Though of course, you shouldn't really go picking them. It was after one of his walks he sat me down for a talk.

"Now then," he started off. It was always going to be a serious conversation when it started with "Now then." "Now then," he says, "You're growing up and starting to become an independent woman." I could feel myself shaking, I thought this was it, here it comes, the sex talk, the worst moment in a child's life and today it's my turn, to be tortured with the graphic details of how to put a condom on a boy or have explained how important it is to get to know each other before you do a 'special kind of hug'. "I don't want us to drift apart," he went on. "So, I want to make an arrangement with you." This sounded ominous. "I want you to pick one day of the week which we'll always spend together. It will be our day. And, in return, you can also pick one other day of the week, where I'll go out and you can have the house to yourself for a few hours." I thought this had to be a trick, surely. But it wasn't. From then on, every Tuesday night we would do something together, and every Thursday night he went out. He'd go to the pub or something and I'd have a bath, play loud music, or just have a friend round.

I'd recently started college. Sciences. Not the most interesting of topics for some people, I know, but I always loved learning about biology. I couldn't decide whether I wanted to be a doctor or vet though, I knew I wanted to do something with living things – helping living things. However, call me naive, but I didn't expect there to be so much reading. I know Thursday was meant to be my day to myself, but I needed to catch up on all my work. I told Dad I was using my Thursday free time to go round my friend's to revise. I'd started researching the human brain for a project and thought it was fascinating! Did you know that, really, multitasking is impossible! What you're actually doing is "context-switching" which means you're not actually doing two things at once. You're just switching your focus really fast between the two. And the short-term memory only lasts about 20 to 30 seconds!

Coming home, I was surprised to find that Dad had locked the front door. He never remembered to lock the door, and he was in, it wasn't as if we were going to get robbed or anything. As soon as I walked in, I could smell fresh flowers. They'd been put in the sink, which really wasn't like Dad. He loved arranging them as soon as he could. I could hear voices coming from the living room, so I headed through. Now I admit, I don't always remember everything exactly as it was, but there are some things I'll never forget. I'll never forget that sofa, for example. I'll never forget the first time I had to dissect a heart in class. And I'll never forget walking in on my Dad laid on top of... (*To a male audience member*) I'm sorry, what's your name? (*Wait for audience members name*) Thank you (*As before*) Laid on top of [NAME] with his hands down his trousers... on that grey sofa.

I can't remember which one of them saw me at the door, or which one of us spoke first, but I do remember [NAME] leaving pretty quickly. I remember him putting on his shoes at the door. And I think I remember Dad kissing him goodbye. I remember a long silence after he left. Though this may have been minutes, it felt like hours. And I can't remember who broke it. But I do remember, amongst other things, Dad saying that [NAME] wasn't the first, and I think I laughed at him and said it was just a mid-life crisis. He said he'd been with men before. Before Mum. And that she always knew. But they didn't see the point in telling me. Why would they? No child needs to know that about their parents. I mean, has anyone ever had *that chat* with their parents before? It's bad enough having the sexual history chat with a partner, let alone a parent! You just know what you see, don't you? And all I ever saw was my Dad with my Mum. I asked if this was why he and Mum split up, but he said it had nothing to do with it. He actually said there was a part of him that still loved Mum and that if she hadn't wanted a divorce, he'd still have been very happy. I asked him about [NAME]. He just smiled.

He was alright, [NAME]. A bit awkward to start with, particularly if we all went out together, but, over the next couple of years, I got to know him. And again, he made Dad happy, which was all I wanted. He was a carer at a nursing home just outside of town. It was in an old, converted church. He really encouraged me to focus on my studies. He said if it was up to him, I should go for being a vet over a doctor any day. "Anything to keep you away from dealing with people!" he'd say.

Pause.

Apparently, elephants can communicate in some really cool ways. They're not dissimilar to humans really. They communicate with each other through touch and body language, and through vibrations in the ground. They can just sense danger or trouble.

I came home from College one Tuesday. All ready for a night in with Dad, just the two of us as always. But when I got home, I could tell there was something wrong. The silence was back, and the flowers were gone. Dad and [NAME] had had an argument about something and Dad seemed to think he wasn't coming back. He was right.

I went off to uni that summer, to study animal medicine. I only applied because of Dad and [NAME]. But now [NAME] was gone, and I was worried about Dad being alone again.

When Dad came to pick me up at the end of the year something was different. He was different. He was smiling again. He couldn't stop smiling the whole way home. He said he had some news to tell me but wanted to wait until we got back to the house. When we walked in, he pointed me to the living room. In there was this beautiful new blue sofa suite. No more grey leather and green felt. It looked amazing. "It was Evie's idea," he said, "We donated the old one to a home."

She was older than I expected, a couple of years older than Dad. She had really deep-set crow's feet – particularly when Dad made her laugh. They made each other laugh a lot.

After she left, Dad was still smiling as he asked me what I thought of her. "I like her," I told him, and I did, I really did, maybe a little louder than I would normally like, but she was nice. "Good," he said, "Cause we're getting married."

She catchers her finger on a thorn and drops the flowers. Pause.

She begins to pick them up and rearrange them.

One   My Dad always used to tell me: "Sometimes, just throwing yourself into something can lead to your most memorable of experiences." Just go for it, basically. I've never thrown myself into things, just gone along with what others have thrown me into. Being exclusive, getting married, moving house, having this carpet, that wallpaper, these shoes, being a fucking sperm donor! Christ! What if I just did what I fucking wanted for once?

He cried when we told him she was pregnant. He cried when we went for the first scan. He cried when we learnt it was going to be a boy, when we felt him kick. And he cried when I told him what I wanted. He cried when I told him I loved him, but I needed more. And he cried when he said "ok", as he said he was fine with that, that I could do what I wanted, that he just didn't want to know about it. I mean let's face it, the honeymoon period was over, and we all know what that means. Too tired, too stressed, got a headache, not tonight Josephine. You know.

Jack's two now. We see him once or twice a week. [NAME] even made us God Parents. It always seems a little weird between us now though. I don't know if that's because of what we did, or because we stopped.

I've started meeting people online now. I follow Chris's rules of course. I never tell him who I meet or what we do, and I never bring them back to the house. I think he likes to believe I'm just working late. Which I sort of am I suppose. I usually meet them at the bridge outside of town, get a bite to eat and then come to the hotel. As I stand on the bridge, waiting for them to pull up, I watch the traffic pass beneath me. And I wonder, what if I jumped? What if I climbed over the railing and just jumped? What would I regret? Would it be my actions themselves or the lies? Then again, I think what if I don't? Sometimes I just come here to the hotel and wait to see if anyone wants to meet up. There's always someone out there lonelier than you.

I never lie to the people I meet. I never hide what I'm doing, I don't avoid talking about Chris or take my wedding ring off or anything like that. Most people are fine with it. You get some people who don't get it, who make assumptions. The way I look at it, it doesn't matter who or what you like, some people can't be with just one person. I do still love Chris. And who knows, whether I was gay or straight, maybe I'd still be doing this.

What if…? (*One's phone pings*) Then again, maybe not today.

One takes one last drink from the mini bar and smartens up his clothes. One exits.

Two   He began to undress me, kissing down my body as he did, then he pushed me on the bed. I watched as he loomed over me. His manly body just… He wasn't quite as muscular as I thought he was going to be, but it was nice, he was homelier, more realistic. No one really wants a Chris Hemsworth; it'd just make you feel shit about yourself the whole time. And let's face it, I'd already had *that* experience. Anyway, he stood over me, touching himself and… he called me beautiful.

He knelt down on the floor at the base of the bed and began going down on me. I'd never actually felt a guy's mouth round me before. I tried desperately not to get too excited as he did it, thinking of the things you think of when you're trying to take things slow. Old geography teachers, the Queen's speech, Shirley Ballas's sweaty cleavage, anything to keep control. I lifted him up to my face to kiss him. I felt him against me as we kissed. Then I felt his hand touching himself. I started jerking off too. I jumped on top of him, straddling him over his thighs. Watching him. Watching him, watching me. We both came at the same time. Fuck me, sex with a guy is messy!

Pause. He puts on a button down shirt.

We showered together afterwards. I'd never even thought about the clean-up… post-coitus as it were. But it made sense. We'd just had the most amazing sex and then washed together. It really finished off the intimacy perfectly. Plus, the hotel had Baylis and Harding shower stuff, so we smelt amazing afterwards too.

He puts on a pair of trousers.

He stayed the whole night. We laid naked together. I never told him, but I actually woke up about an hour before him, and I just watched him sleep. It was amazing. And when he eventually woke up... He. Fucked. Me. So, hard. I mean seriously, as soon as his eyes opened and he smiled at me, I just wanted it. I think he was a little scared at first to be honest. I just jumped on top of him and started kissing him and touching him, but then he reached for the Durex that we'd put on the bedside table the night before, just in case, ripped it open with his teeth and before I knew it, it was on him. It was proper like a porno, where you never actually see them put it on but then suddenly it's there. And my god, I thought it felt big in my mouth! I can't imagine what would have happened if I'd have let the first guy fuck me with his!

He puts on a pair of smart shoes that go well with his outfit.

We started with me sat on top him, his hands all over my body. Then he flipped me onto the bed, on my side, like spooning and I felt his whole body wrapped around me, really engulfing me. When he came, he was on top, my legs spread as wide as I could so that he could lean down and kiss me. And he was looking at me. I mean really looking right at me. Dead in the eyes. It may have started with him just fucking me but, and I know this is going to sound all wet and mushy or whatever but, by the end he wasn't just fucking me. We were making love.

Pause. He puts on a jacket or blazer, checks his hair and teeth.

He is ready for his date.

Did I look alright? Did I smell alright? Did he fancy me? Did I have something stuck in my teeth? Did I fucking care? Sure, sure, sure, I paid for [NAME] to take me out to dinner, I paid him to come back to my hotel room, I paid him to wash with me, and I paid him to fuck me till I came. But I didn't pay him to make love to me. And I'm not at all ashamed for paying for the other stuff because it was worth it. So the next time you can't be arsed, and you choose Deliveroo over cooking it for yourself, just stop for a second... and think of me having the best fuck of my life.

Two *exits.*

Three   Dad and Evie had been married about 6 months when Dad had his car accident. He was in a coma for about a week. While he was out, they did some scans. It seems, when he had the accident, he also had a stroke.

Pause.

The reason they say an elephant never forgets, is because of its temporal lobe. The area of the brain that's associated with the memory. It's larger than a humans, and denser, so they can hold information better.

When you have a stroke, the blood flow to the brain is affected. Sometimes its reduced, sometimes it just stops for a bit. This means that your brain isn't getting the oxygen it needs. It only takes a few minutes without oxygen for the brain to start to die.

It was Dad's temporal lobe that was most starved of oxygen.

She phoned me up one day, Evie. She said the Doctor had just been. "Dementia." Apparently, a stroke can bring it on and bring it on fast. When I told Mum she burst into tears. Carl tried to comfort her which, to be fair, he did instantly, but you could see he was confused as to why she was this upset about her ex-husband. That's loyalty for you.

No one ever tells you what it's really like. People think it's just a case of forgetting a few names, or where you've put things. Mobile phone in the fridge, car keys in the kettle, that sort of thing. No one ever tells you just how hard it is. Forgetting your wife's face. Not knowing when you need to eat. I watched Dad become someone else. Someone I didn't know. I watched as his eyes clouded over, as he no longer responded to my voice, as he flinched away from me for fear of who I might be. I'd spent all my life wanting him to be happy, wanting him not to be alone. But this time there was nothing I could do, and I couldn't even talk to Dad about it. I had no one I could talk to about it, about me, about how I was feeling. No one ever asked how I was feeling. No one ever asked about me! I'm sorry, sorry. This isn't about me, is it? No.

Evie couldn't look after him by herself anymore. She'd done her best, she really had. But she was a wife, not a carer. And you could see her heart break a little each time he called her by Mum's name by mistake. As I stood at the old arched wooden doors of the ex-church-come-care home, I could feel something inside me. Something familiar. I went in to visit Dad and when I walked in this feeling got stronger, and then I saw them. Dad, Evie and [NAME], all sat together on the old grey sofa, with the smell of flowers all around him. And he was happy again.

When he passed away... Evie, [NAME], Mum and I all sat together – the loyal, sociable elephants we had become. I cried. I remember I cried a lot. As we walked through the garden of remembrance, there was a girl sorting out the flowers. She must have seen the tears on my face because the next thing I know, I can feel her hand on mine. She looked at me and smiled a comforting smile, her blue eyes looking straight through me. "Are you gonna be alright?" she asked.

This is where my story begins.

Three *picks up her flowers and exits.* **END**